THE INSIDER'S GUIDE TO FISHING

ICE FISHING

LIKE A PRO

MARIE ROESSER

Rosen
PUBLISHING

Published in 2024 by The Rosen Publishing Group, Inc.
2544 Clinton Street, Buffalo, NY 14224

Copyright © 2024 by The Rosen Publishing Group, Inc.

Portions of this work were originally authored by Bridget Heos and published as *Ice Fishing*. All new material in this edition was authored by Marie Roesser.

Editor: Therese M. Shea
Designer: Michael Flynn

All rights reserved. No part of this book may be reproduced in any form without permission in writing from the publisher, except by a reviewer.

Library of Congress Cataloging-in-Publication Data

Names: Roesser, Marie, author.
Title: Ice fishing like a pro / Marie Roesser.
Description: Buffalo, New York : Rosen Publishing, [2024] | Series: The insider's guide to fishing | Includes bibliographical references and index.
Identifiers: LCCN 2023036172 (print) | LCCN 2023036173 (ebook) | ISBN 9781499476040 (library binding) | ISBN 9781499476033 (paperback) | ISBN 9781499476057 (ebook)
Subjects: LCSH: Ice fishing--Juvenile literature.
Classification: LCC SH455.345 .R64 2023 (print) | LCC SH455.45 (ebook) | DDC 799.12/2--dc23/eng/20230817
LC record available at https://lccn.loc.gov/2023036172
LC ebook record available at https://lccn.loc.gov/2023036173

Some of the images in this book illustrate individuals who are models. The depictions do not imply actual situations or events.

Manufactured in the United States of America

CPSIA Compliance Information: Batch #CWRYA24. For further information, contact Rosen Publishing at 1-800-237-9932.

CONTENTS

INTRODUCTION 4

CHAPTER 1
WHERE TO ICE FISH SAFELY 6

CHAPTER 2
ICE FISHING EQUIPMENT 24

CHAPTER 3
READY FOR THE ICE 40

CHAPTER 4
FINDING YOUR FISH 54

GLOSSARY 74

FOR FURTHER READING 75

FOR MORE INFORMATION 76

INDEX 78

ABOUT THE AUTHOR/CONSULTANT 80

INTRODUCTION

Fishing can be a magical activity. At least, it sometimes seems like it takes a bit of magic to coax a catch out of the water. But when you do get a fish on the hook, the real magic of fishing seems clear. That feeling of excitement when a fish tugs on the rod is what every angler is looking for.

Ice fishing might be the most mysterious form of fishing. After all, the window to the underwater world is just a small hole in the ice. Beginner's luck can get the fish biting, of course, but many people who ice fish use a lot of knowledge to keep reeling them in. Some of it is ancient knowledge. According to evidence, Native peoples have been ice fishing at least as far back as 2,000 years ago—likely they were on the ice a lot longer than that, though. We know they used holes in the ice, spears, and small rods, not too different from what's used today. It wasn't too long ago that this sport was updated for modern times with technology, including sonar and power tools. But some still swear by just using their angler's intuition.

Perhaps more than any other kind of fishing, ice fishing really does require some research before heading out on the "hard water," as some ice fishers call the ice. Even just a bit of research can save a life. Ice fishing can be dangerous for those who don't understand the nature of the ice they're relying on to hold them. But after reading a bit, inquiring with local fishing agencies, and gathering a few other ice-fishing enthusiasts—including someone with experience—an ice-fishing novice will be ready for first ice. This is the start of ice-fishing season, when the ice is several inches thick and clear as glass.

Today's ice fishing, for some, is less about fishing for food and more about friendships on the ice. Whether fishers are holed up together in a fancy shelter or sitting on an overturned bucket out in the open, striking up conversations about what's biting what bait and when happen frequently. That's how more seasoned anglers pass on their tried-and-true techniques to younger ones.

Some people, however, need to ice fish as a way to find fish for food. These fishers get to know where the fish they're seeking like to lurk in colder weather and what kind of bait will attract them. In Minnesota, walleye is the most sought-after fish. In Wisconsin, the 16-day sturgeon spearing season is highly anticipated. Alaskans catch inland salmon, while anglers in the Northwest tend to aim for trout. In the Northeast, bass, perch, pike, and many other fish species are worth the wait in the cold. Canadian waters are prime territory for all these and more. Both larger game fish and smaller panfish seem to be tastier coming out of freezing waters. Whether you're an expert who grew up on the ice or are new to the hard water, this book will help you learn how to perfect your ice-fishing methods.

CHAPTER 1
WHERE TO ICE FISH SAFELY

Ice fishing is a fun and exciting sport but one that requires even more caution than normal around the water. That's because the kind of ice that people should fish on doesn't form well everywhere. The area where conditions are usually good for ice fishing during winter is sometimes called the ice belt. In North America, this includes all of Canada and south to the U.S. states that are north of 40 degrees north latitude, such as Washington, Idaho, Nebraska, and Pennsylvania. Even south of that zone, temperatures in some places may get cold enough for ice fishing, particularly in high elevation areas. For example, some lakes in New Mexico and California can be ice-fishing spots during cold winters.

ICE-FISHING DESTINATIONS

Perhaps the most popular ice-fishing region is the Great Lakes. The Great Lakes themselves are too big to freeze over, but some of the bays get good ice. More commonly, people fish on smaller lakes and ponds in the states and provinces around the Great Lakes.

Minnesota is home to the most ice anglers in the United States. There, tens of thousands of ice shelters are pulled onto lakes each year—about 5,000 on Mille Lacs alone. People typically fish for walleye, which are large game fish, and smaller panfish, such as perch. Competitions like the Eelpout Festival on Leech Lake honor anglers who catch the biggest or most fish.

Ice fishing is also extremely popular in Michigan and Wisconsin. Each year, ice fishing takes place on many of Michigan's 11,000 lakes. Houghton Lake is the largest inland lake in the state and is host to Tip-Up Town USA, a winter festival featuring ice fishing and other cold-weather

WHERE TO ICE FISH SAFELY 9

Ice fishing is one of the most popular winter sports in Minnesota.

activities, such as a polar bear dip (where people run into the freezing water in their swimsuits). In Wisconsin, anglers fish for the usual game fish and panfish. They also have a unique tradition: spearfishing for sturgeon, a fish that has existed 120 million years and can grow to be more than 200 pounds (90.7 kilograms).

Many lakes in New York don't enjoy the thick ice of Minnesota, Wisconsin, or Michigan, but New Yorkers still have ice-fishing options. The bays of Lake Ontario and Adirondack waters such as Lake Champlain and Lake George are especially beautiful. Here, anglers may even be able to score some salmon, a difficult catch.

Permanent ice houses like this one in Canada are rigged for heat and other comforts.

Though New England is close to the Atlantic Ocean, it has long, cold winters. The jet stream's movement in the winter means low-pressure systems pull cold, dry air down from Canada. In Maine, winter is known as the time of year when locals take back the waterfront. Many wealthy people summer in Maine. But in the winter, local ice anglers pull shanties onto the ice. They're not trespassing, because the Great Ponds Act states that lakes over 10 acres (0.04 square kilometer) are public property. Most northern states have similar laws granting public rights to navigable waters.

West of the Great Lake states, the Badlands and Black Hills of South Dakota offer trout fishing opportunities, especially in the Black Hills National Forest's Sheridan Lake, Deerfield Reservoir, and Pactola Reservoir. Because of Deerfield's high elevation, anglers can often ice fish for longer than elsewhere in the state. The lake has rainbow and brook trout and splake (a cross between brook trout and lake trout). Devils Lake and Lake Metigoshe are two of the most popular places to ice fish in North Dakota. Lake Metigoshe is one of the cleanest natural freshwater lakes in that state. The Dakotas also have some off-the-beaten-path lakes that can only be accessed by skis or snowmobile.

Farther west, anglers can try their luck in the snow-fed lakes of the Rocky Mountains of Montana, Wyoming, Utah, and Colorado. Montana, in particular, has some huge lakes that are suitable for ice fishing. Flathead Lake, the largest natural freshwater lake in the western United States by surface area, is too big to freeze, but its bays do. Fort Peck Lake, a reservoir in northeast Montana, is 250,000 acres (1,011 sq km) and 220 feet (67 meters) deep. It is home to more than 50 kinds of fish.

Ice fishing has become more popular in Colorado in recent years. The Department of Fish and Wildlife's hatchery program stocks lakes and reservoirs in late fall. That means many favorite Colorado fish, such as rainbow trout, brook trout, cutthroat trout, and kokanee salmon, are available in the winter too. Among the best-known lakes for ice fishing are Georgetown Lake, Eleven Mile Reservoir, Harvey Gap Reservoir, and Evergreen Lake.

Much farther west and north, Alaska is known for its salmon fishing—both in summer and winter. Chinook and kokanee salmon are common fish caught through the ice as well as Dolly Varden char and arctic char.

This is a Dolly Varden char. Its name comes from a character in the Charles Dickens novel *Barnaby Rudge*.

WHERE TO ICE FISH SAFELY

Finally, ice fishers have Canada, where nearly the entire country is ice-fishing territory. As in Alaska, even parts of the ocean freeze, so you can ice fish on saltwater inlets. Quebec, for instance, has one of the largest saltwater ice-fishing villages in the world: Pêche Blanche du Fjord. There, people ice fish for redfish, cod, and rainbow smelt, among others. But ice fishing on lakes, such as Lake Nipissing and Lake Simcoe in the province of Ontario, is more common. Lake Simcoe, an hour north of Toronto, hosts the annual Canadian ice-fishing championship and is considered the ice-fishing capital of North America. Every winter, 4,000 shelters go up on the lake, where yellow perch is a popular catch.

Now that you know where to fish, let's focus on the single most important thing you need to know before getting out on the hard water: safety.

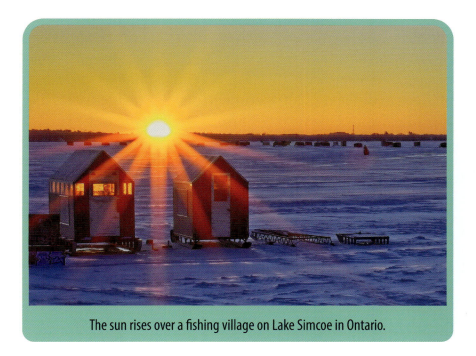

The sun rises over a fishing village on Lake Simcoe in Ontario.

SAFETY FIRST

If you've ever watched the popular long-running TV show *Deadliest Catch*, you know that falling into frigid water is a big deal. Within minutes, you can lose consciousness just because of the cold. Add a ceiling of ice to the equation, especially if you're in moving water, and you've got a dangerous situation. So, when it comes to ice fishing, preventing falls through the ice is the top priority.

The first thing to know is that not all ice is the same. That's right; there are different kinds of ice and they have different strengths. Newer, clear ice is the strongest. White and snow-covered ice is not as strong. The recommendations below are based on new, clear ice. When ice fishing on white and snowy ice, double all measurements for maximum safety.

First, you should ALWAYS fish with someone else, never alone. When ice fishing with a small group, the ice should be at least 4 to 5 inches (10 to 13 cm) deep. It can be trickier to ice fish on rivers with heavy currents. Thicknesses can vary with just a few steps. That's why many anglers avoid rivers altogether. However, large rivers like the Mississippi have bays and backwaters that are still enough to create safe conditions.

To drive a car or small truck on ice, you'll need at least 15 inches (38 cm). Keep in mind that shock waves due to pressure from vehicles and natural elements like underwater springs can weaken the ice. Standard advice is to drive with windows down, doors unlocked, seatbelts off, and a hand on the door handle. Survival rates are low for drivers and passengers who fall through the ice. Don't risk driving (or riding in a car) on thin ice.

WHERE TO ICE FISH SAFELY   15

To drive a snowmobile or ATV (all-terrain vehicle) on ice, you'll need around 5 or 6 inches (13 to 15 cm) of clear ice.

Before you walk onto a lake, you should stop at a bait shop, park lodge, or another place where you can find information about ice conditions. You should always check for yourself too. As you walk out onto the lake, particularly during first and late ice, you should test the depth periodically by chiseling a hole and using a tape measure. You can use an ice chisel, ice auger, or even a cordless drill with a long bit. Then tap the ice to test for hollowness. A hollow sound indicates that the water level has dropped. Ice isn't stable in this case because water isn't supporting it.

Once you determine that the ice is relatively safe, continue to proceed with caution. Keep in mind that 4 inches (10 cm) of ice in one spot can be 3 inches (8 cm) just a few feet away. Shore ice freezes first, so the ice might thin as you go farther out onto a lake or bay. Pick at the ice in front of you with your spud (a long chisel) to feel for unstable spots. Continue to measure the depth as you go farther away from shore.

Because ice can vary and change, it's important to understand what affects ice thickness. First, there are geographical conditions. Bodies of water that are close to the ocean typically freeze later than those farther inland. The ocean stores heat from the summer sun. So the wind blowing off the relatively warm sea is warmer than wind blowing inland. With maritime winds typically blowing west to east, the Pacific Northwest and Europe get frozen waters at much higher latitude than elsewhere in the world. However, even New England lakes freeze later the closer they are to the ocean.

Next, consider the lake itself. Deep water and water covering a large area freeze later—if at all. Not only do large bodies of water retain heat better than smaller bodies of water, they also have stronger currents (moving water

WHERE TO ICE FISH SAFELY   17

An auger that a fisher uses looks a bit like a large drill.

freezes at lower temperatures than still water) and blowing winds. For these reasons, the main bodies of the Great Lakes almost never freeze, though their bays and lagoons may. The ocean freezes closer to the poles and at lower temperatures. Rivers, which move very quickly, are also slower to freeze. Rivers pose an additional danger to ice fishers. If you fall through the ice, you can be swiftly carried downstream and away from the hole you drilled. Only venture out on an icy river with extreme caution.

MORE SAFETY CONCERNS

Aside from ice thickness, here are a few more ice-fishing safety considerations:

- Hypothermia and frostbite. Clothing will be discussed in the next chapter, but the main idea is to layer and be prepared. Be aware that windchill can make an air temperature of 20°Fahrenheit (-7°Celsius) feel like -22°F (-30°C). Getting wet, either from sweat or precipitation, will make you colder. Bring a dry set of clothes. Have hot liquids ready to drink. Also, know the body of water you're on and take extra care not to get lost in a storm.

- Falls. Avoid falls on slippery ice by wearing boots with good traction or creepers, which are shoe spikes you can put over your boots. When walking, keep your hands free to catch yourself. Cover sharp objects such as auger blades when you move them to avoid injuries if you fall.

- Fire safety and carbon monoxide concerns. If you're in a shelter with a heater, avoid carbon monoxide poisoning by having two sources of ventilation that are unclogged. For fire safety, don't lock shelters from the inside.

WHERE TO ICE FISH SAFELY   19

In popular ice-fishing spots, authorities may put up warning signs about the conditions of the ice. Always believe them.

A body of water also has features that can make the ice thinner in some places. This is especially true of large irregular lakes, which don't freeze uniformly. These features include underwater springs, creeks flowing into the lake, and patches of snow, which can insulate ice, making it warmer. Ice around objects frozen into the ice—such as boats or leaf piles—can also be unstable. Any lake in which the water level varies (such as those used for irrigation or power) should not be considered stable.

Varying conditions include sunlight, wind, and other weather conditions. A shaded lake will freeze earlier than a sunny one. Lakes exposed to wind freeze later. Early and late in the season, when the ice is at its thinnest, temperatures above freezing (32°F [0°C]) for six hours of the day can weaken the ice. Temperatures above freezing for 24 hours or more mean the ice is no longer safe, unless it's midwinter and the ice is very thick.

Even if someone knows the ice, accidents can happen. If you do fall through, don't panic. Face the direction you came from. Climb onto the ice. If that ice breaks, keep trying until you find stable ice. Once you're out of the water, don't stand. Instead, roll to land. Change into dry clothes, and seek medical attention.

If the person you're with falls through the ice, you'll need to help them without becoming a victim yourself. Don't run to the hole because more ice could collapse. Instead, throw or extend an item such as a rope or skis to the friend. Once out of the water, get your friend into dry clothes. Seek medical help. Even if they think they feel fine, hypothermia can set in later.

WHERE TO ICE FISH SAFELY 21

Two trucks fell through the ice of a Minnesota lake after a brief thaw in the winter.

22 ICE FISHING LIKE A PRO

Many women's fishing clubs provide mentors, or experienced teachers, who act as advisors for beginners.

LET'S TALK TERMS

You might notice in this book that the term "fisherman" isn't used. That's because women ice fish too. While some women who fish prefer the term "fishermen," others say it excludes women. Scientific writing about fishing uses the term "fishers" for all people who fish, and this is the term mostly used in this text. However, you may also see the word "angler," which means someone who fishes with a rod and line. Most fishers on the ice get their fish this way. Others use spears to catch their fish, though, so angler isn't a term that would accurately include them.

So, how many women fish? In the United States, more than one-third of all fishers are women, and in Canada, one-fifth of all fishers are women. While ice fishers in particular were mostly men for a long time, the makeup of the sport is changing. Overall ice fisher numbers are difficult to know because many fishing licenses are year-round, but more fishing clubs just for women are being established, such as Ontario Women Anglers and Wisconsin Women Fish. The Women Ice Angler Project, founded in 2015, promotes women ice anglers and ice-fishing organizations across the United States and Canada. It seeks more and better representation for women within the fishing industry as a whole and particularly in ice fishing.

CHAPTER 2

ICE FISHING EQUIPMENT

Packing the right equipment is especially important with ice fishing. You have to pack a mix of gear for the sport and gear to keep you and your group safe. If something goes wrong, running back to land to get gear might not be possible. And if something goes right—and you snag a fish—you need to have what you require to reel it in.

THE ESSENTIALS

Perhaps the most essential pieces of equipment are tools to test the ice thickness. Most experienced ice fishers use a spud bar, which is a type of ice chisel. It's usually made of steel and about 4 or 5 feet (1.2 to 1.5 m) long. Some fishers walk along the ice banging the spud against the surface. As they do this, they listen for changes that might indicate weak spots in the ice.

Next, you'll need a tape measure and something to cut a hole in the ice. Technically, you could cut the hole with the spud, but it's much easier to use an auger. An auger looks like a giant corkscrew. With a manual auger, you turn it into the ice yourself, which is labor-intensive, especially if the ice is very thick.

Many people today use a gasoline-powered auger so they can quickly drill multiple holes. Power augers were introduced around World War II (1939–1945) but didn't become affordable, reliable, and lightweight until the mid-1980s. At that point, they helped revolutionize ice fishing. They allowed people to fish several holes rather than chiseling out one and hoping for the best. You can think of holes in the ice as the equivalent of casts onto the water—you try a few until you find the fish.

Power augers come in various sizes. A 5-inch (13 cm) auger works for panfish, whereas 8 to 10 inches (20 to

ICE FISHING EQUIPMENT   27

The ice-fishing hole can be made larger with the spud bar if the auger's hole seems too small.

25 cm) might be necessary for larger game fish. Deeper ice requires more horsepower. Power augers cost in the range of $200 to $600. The blades can be kept sharp with sharpening stones. To keep the hole clear after you drill, you'll need a simple tool called a skimmer. It helps scoop icy slush out of the hole.

So now you have your spot on the ice and your entrance into the water. Next you'll need ice-fishing rods—called jigging rods. (Jigging is a type of vertical fishing where you use a type of lure called a jig.) Like other modern fishing rods, ice rods are made of graphite or fiberglass. However, ice rods are shorter than standard fishing rods. This is because when your line goes straight down into the water and you need to muscle a fish out of a small hole, a long pole can be unwieldy. Ice rods vary in weight from ultra-light (for fishing panfish), to light (for panfish or small game fish), to heavy (for larger game fish). A heavier rod can bring in a big fish, but a lighter rod allows you to move the lure more effectively and feel bites more easily.

For light rods, a light reel is needed to achieve higher sensitivity—a necessity in winter when the fish tend to bite less heartily. The spool doesn't have to be very long, since ice fishing doesn't require casting and you won't likely fish more than 20 to 50 feet (6 to 15 m) deep. However, allow for some extra line in case the fish runs, and make sure the reel has good drag. (The fish should be able to take some line, and you should be able to set the hook without breaking the line.)

The fishing line should stand up under harsh winter weather. Monofilament or fluorocarbon is best. Match your test line to the fish you're trying to catch: panfish, 4- to 6-pound (2 to 3 kg) test line; trout, 6-pound (3 kg) test line; and pike and other game fish, 12- to 14-pound (5 to 6 kg)

ICE FISHING EQUIPMENT 29

Ice-fishing rods are typically 18 to 48 inches (46 to 122 cm) long.

An advantage of fluorocarbon line is that it can look nearly invisible to fish in clear waters, but monofilament is often stronger.

test line. For bigger fish, you may need 20- to 80-pound (9 to 36 kg) test line. Test means the amount of weight that can be applied to the line before it breaks. A steel leader may be needed when pursuing larger fish with sharp teeth.

Ice fishers also use special fishing contraptions called tip-ups. They're also called ice traps, fish traps, or tilts. These are like a fishing rod, only without the rod. They simply have a spool and line attached to a base. You set the tip-up directly over the hole. A flag goes up when you get a bite. Then you set the tip-up aside and pull the line up by hand. You can buy handcrafted wooden tip-ups or manufactured polar tip-ups. They allow fishers to set and watch several baited lines. Most places have limits on the number of tip-ups you can use, such as four per fisher.

Generally, you use bait for tip-ups and lures for jigs (perhaps tipped with bait). This is because you can move your jig, making the lure move according to its design. But tip-ups are left alone in the water, so the movement of the minnow or other live bait is needed to attract the fish. Allow your live bait to move naturally by hooking it the right way. Minnows should be hooked through their backs, for instance. For worms, it's a good idea to hook one all the way through and then tip the hook with a squirming live worm.

Different lures and bait work for different situations. In general, clear water calls for natural-looking lures, whereas dark water requires flashier—even phosphorescent—lures. Small lures work for panfish, whereas

When the line attached to this tip-up snags a fish, the flag raises to alert the fisher.

big lures—3 to 6 inches (8 to 15 cm)—are better for game fish. It's also best to match the lure to the natural food of the fish you're pursuing. If the fish eats plankton, small lures are best. If the fish eats other fish, the lure should at least resemble fish. Moving lures, such as spinners, are effective.

As far as bait, game fish go after large minnows or golden shiners, whereas panfish like larvae or small minnows. For dark waters, you can buy euro larvae—live bait dyed bright colors. Larvae can be kept warm by keeping them in a container in your pocket. You can keep minnows from freezing in the bucket by using a small aerator for the water.

Hook size varies according to fish size but also according to the size of the fish's mouth. A treble hook is good for keepers, but they can injure fish you intend to set free. Barbless hooks might be better for catch and release.

If you plan to keep the fish, you'll want to bring a gaff (a handled hook for lifting heavier fish). Once the fish is close to the hole, you can hook it with the gaff and pull it through the hole. But if you're going to release the fish, the gaff may hurt it. You'll need to pull the fish in with your hands instead.

Bobbers can be used to show when you get a bite and measure water depth. (If you know where the fish are, you can keep dropping your line to that spot.)

Other supplies you'll need include tools for cutting the line or making minor repairs, large buckets for supplies and bringing home fish, nets for getting bait out of the bucket, and something to transport everything. This can be as simple as a child's sled or as high tech as an ice-fishing container that doubles as a portable shelter. You can pull it by hand, with a snowmobile or ATV, or, on very thick ice, a truck.

ICE FISHING EQUIPMENT 33

Young anglers pull their ice-fishing gear easily on the ice with a sled.

SHELTERS AND MORE

The St. Paul Ice Fishing Show is the largest in the United States and attracts thousands of shoppers. Here, you can find some of the most innovative ice-fishing supplies in the world. These include the portable ice shelter.

On very cold days, a shelter allows anglers to brave the elements more safely and more comfortably. In the past, permanent shelters were moved on and off the lake once a year. They were too heavy to move more often than that. If the fish weren't biting beneath the shelter, there wasn't much you could do. With the invention of the portable shelter, however, fishers can now drill some holes,

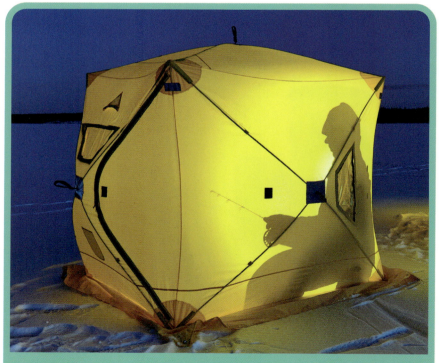

There are many kinds of portable ice shelters. Those made of heavier materials can withstand stronger winds but are harder to transport.

ICE FISHING EQUIPMENT 35

An ice shelter can be much more comfortable than sitting out on the ice, especially in bad weather.

see where the fish are biting, and set up the shelter there. It's lightweight and easy to set up and take down.

Some people still opt for permanent shelters, however, perhaps because they provide a sense of home. You can paint one a bright color, put in a well-ventilated propane or wood-burning stove, and add some comforts of home. If it's atop a hole, you can actually fish there. If not, it can serve as a home base. Most ice shelters are pretty bare—paneling serves as insulation; windows, if required, are cut out; and a table and chairs create a dinner spot. However, some high-end models have TVs, leather couches, and more luxuries.

DAVE GENZ: MR. ICE FISHING

Dave Genz is considered the father of modern ice fishing. He pioneered the mobile, flexible style of ice fishing used today rather than the "sit at one hole and wait" style of yesteryear.

Genz came from a family of Minnesota ice fishers. His father, a construction engineer with time off in the winter, fished Mille Lacs in Minnesota. Genz followed in his footsteps. A maintenance engineer for a linen company, Genz was welding together a portable shelter one day when another engineer asked, "What is that?" Genz said it was a "fish trap," and that's how his ice shelter got its name.

Genz also developed what's now called the Vexilar Genz Pack, a portable sonar holder, bringing the use of sonar into ice fishing. He even made the first modern graphite ice-fishing rod.

Genz, the first professional ice fisherman in the world, was inducted into the Minnesota Fishing Hall of Fame in 2002. In 2010, he was inducted into the National Fresh Water Fishing Hall of Fame for making a "lasting national or world impact to the benefit of freshwater sportfishing."

Even with a shelter, you'll need to dress warmly. Layers are key. Specifically, you'll want the first layer to wick away sweat and other moisture, the second to warm you, and the third to block the wind. If it's snowing, you might also want a waterproof shell. These items can be found at most outdoor clothing stores. Some gear is specific to ice fishing, including clothes with big zippers (so that you can shed layers when your fingers are numb), pants with knee pads, gloves that stay warm when wet, and boots rated to

ICE FISHING EQUIPMENT

-150°F (-101°C). These items are great for midwinter trips, but on warmer days, a hoodie might suffice (though you should pack heavier clothes too). You'll always need plenty of gloves, especially if you're wrestling large fish out of a hole. Bring several pairs in a sealable plastic bag.

Another important comfort is warm food. Fried fish fillets and potatoes are a typical lunch. You can deep-fry your fish and potatoes with a fish cooker, or simply fry them in a pan over a wood or gas stove. You may also want to

Ice fishing doesn't only happen in rural areas. This ice-fishing village is on the St. Lawrence River in Montreal, Canada.

bring things to do—skates, snowshoes, a football—anything to stay moving and keep warm. However, if you, or the people nearby, are serious about fishing, don't make a lot of noise. It scares off the fish.

Finally, for ice anglers willing to invest extra money in the catch of the day, several gadgets will help locate fish. These include a depth finder, which is helpful because fish often feed in shallows or at drop-offs. To use a depth finder (which looks like a flashlight), you clear away snow and set the unit directly on the ice. The depth finder tells you the water depth. For more information about the bottom of the lake, you can buy a special fishing GPS. This is like a regular GPS, only it allows you to download contour maps that show underwater features like drop-offs, shoals (underwater sandbanks), and sunken islands. Finally, fish finders use sonar pulses to allow you to see where the actual fish are! Fish show up as lines or colors on the screen, allowing you to lower your lines to the correct depth and revise your presentation if the fish are there but not biting. Fish finders range in price from less than $100 to several thousand dollars. You can even purchase an underwater camera and view the fish you're trying to catch as if it's on television!

Many of these gadgets are expensive. Keep in mind that they're a luxury—not a necessity—for ice fishers. Ice fishing is a relatively cheap sport. Less high-tech methods of finding fish include studying a lake map, searching for weeds that have drifted to the surface, or talking to bait shop workers and other anglers. Remember, thousands of years ago, people fished with nothing but a spear—and they counted on their success to feed themselves and their families.

SAFETY GEAR

You can also pack ice-fishing equipment that may help keep you safe—or even save a life. A life vest can be worn under your outerwear. (It should be noted that people in enclosed vehicles like trucks are cautioned not to wear floatation devices as they may hinder them getting out of the car in case of an accident on the ice.) Some kinds of suits (sometimes called float suits) work as flotation devices in case the wearer ends up in the water. Ice picks can be used to achieve a good grip on the ice and pull yourself up if you fall through ice. That's why most experienced anglers hang them around their neck or tuck them in a belt or pocket. Another safety device is called a throw bag. It's simply a long rope stuffed into a bag that can be thrown to someone in the water.

In addition to these, people who travel in more remote areas should have a device with GPS or at least a compass so they know where they are at all times. In areas with poor connections to cell phone towers, special radio communication devices can help anglers talk to each other or make a connection with the Coast Guard.

Ice cleats, or creepers, are spikes that can be fixed to the bottom of shoes or boots. They help anglers keep a grip on the ice when walking and avoid twisting their ankles.

Finally, don't forget a first aid kit! A lot can happen on the ice, including hooking yourself by accident. Even a small first aid kit will come in handy at some point in your fishing career.

CHAPTER 3
READY FOR THE ICE

So you have your ice-fishing gear. You're warmly dressed. You have a group of friends. You have a plan to make a fishing hole on safe ice. What's next? You need to do some research about the regulations of fishing where you live. People who don't follow the regulations may have to pay fines. But most of these regulations are meant to keep fishers safe, the fish populations healthy, and the environment clean for everyone.

LICENSES AND MORE

Before you head to hard water, you might need a fishing license. Every U.S. state and Canadian province has different rules about who needs a license. Some younger fishers might not need one at all. It's easy to check these regulations online. Your state or provincial fish and wildlife agency will have the best, most up-to-date information. If you do need a license, you probably can apply for it online too. The good news is that you don't need a special ice-fishing license. So, any fishing you want to do other times of the year will be covered. Licenses aren't usually much money, and the fees often go back to conservation efforts.

Another regulation to research is whether ice fishing is allowed where you want to go. A lake that has fishing in the summer might not permit ice fishing in the winter. If you do find a place that allows ice fishing, look for special rules such as the number of tip-ups a fisher is allowed, the kinds of lures, hooks, and bait permitted, and the number, size, and species of fish that can be caught. A park or local wildlife agency's website may have this information.

Environmental rules are another consideration. Keep the area around your fishing site clean. Be sure to pick up trash before it blows away. Also, plan to throw

Your fishing license, or permit, might look like this.

back fish that you won't eat as well as large fish required to maintain the population. In the winter, catch-and-release can be tricky. Dropping fish on the ice can hurt them. Even handling them too much can remove their slimy layer, which protects them from infection. Finally, the hook itself can damage their mouth, decreasing their ability to survive in the wild.

If you plan to throw back fish, pull in the fish gently—with your hands, not a gaff. Keep the fish off the ground. Carefully remove the hook, and get the fish back in the water as soon as possible. You'll probably have time to snap a picture but not enough time to carry it around to show others. Set it in the water head first, and hold it there for a minute. It will be tired (like how we feel after holding our breath). Once it is moving again, gently release it.

44 ICE FISHING LIKE A PRO

Ice fishers who use shelters should research regulations about them. Follow rules about locks, windows, ventilation, and the date shelters need to be removed from the ice.

STUDY YOUR LAKE

The next step to ice fishing is to know your lake or whatever body of water you're on. Get a map with contours and find out where the structures—or features—are. Structures or features are parts of the lake that aren't uniform. Some lakes have mounds of land, like underwater islands, at their bottom, for example. (Some people sink old trees or shrubs in strategic places before the lake freezes to create fish-attracting structures.) Another example is a drop-off leading from shallow to deep water.

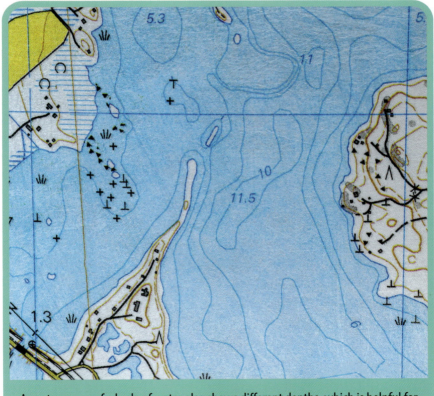

A contour map of a body of water also shows different depths, which is helpful for pursuing kinds of fish that prefer certain depths.

Next, talk to fishery departments, bait shop workers, and other anglers. Different lakes are known for different fish. For instance, in Michigan, Saginaw Bay is known for its walleyes, Hamlin Lake for perch, and Higgins Lake for smelt. There is even a part of Higgins Lake known as Smeltville, where fishers seek this small but tasty fish. Some fishers have created online message boards discussing where you can find out what is biting and when. But don't be afraid to try your own spot based on an educated guess. Have a game plan for places you want to fish, but be flexible.

Fish follow both seasonal and daily migration patterns. Early in the ice-fishing season, panfish start out in weedy shallows, about 15 feet (4.6 m) deep, in search of food. Later in winter, they retreat to deep water flats—about 30 feet (9 m) down. They like to hang out at drop-offs or near structures such as sunken islands. They return to shallows to feed—but not as far into the shallows. In late ice, they return more frequently and go farther into the shallows.

No matter the time of year, fish tend to move daily from deeper water structures to shallow water to feed. This route may be along a weed line or a structure such as a reef. It may also be along a sharply sloping shore, which makes for a quick route. There might be an area along the route where they'll find food or cover. This might be the first break line, or drop, between shallow and deep water.

Game fish hunt panfish, so they tend to be where the panfish are, only slightly deeper. Both panfish and game fish hide out around structures including reefs, stone walls, sunken islands, points, and lagoons. Combination structures, such as weeds and rubble, are especially attractive to fish. If you have sonar, you can use it to further pinpoint lake features and where the fish are. If you find a hot spot, use your GPS to record the coordinates. It will probably be a good fishing hole on other days too.

In addition to migrating, fish tend to bite more zealously at certain times of the day and certain parts of the season. Winter fish generally feed at the same time as they do in the summer, so a dusk-and-dawn summer fish is also a dusk-and-dawn winter fish. Season-wise, early ice and late ice are known to be good times to fish.

CLIMATE CHANGE

Climate change is the phrase used for long-term shifts in temperatures and weather patterns. Global warming, the increase in Earth's temperatures, is a part of these shifts. You've probably heard about both these terms on the news. Climate change affects ice fishing too, especially the safety of the ice. Places where fishers could once rely on consistently cold weather in February are experiencing warming temperatures at times, for example. Even if these temperatures plunge again, the ice is affected and may no longer be suitable to support fishing.

A study published in 2022 in the scientific journal *Nature* suggests that global warming will continue to reduce the thickness of lake ice and the number of days it lasts on the surface. These changes will have a very real impact on the sport of ice fishing—and it seems they already have in some places. In 2023, annual ice fishing derbies on Lake Champlain in Vermont were cancelled in February because of higher than normal temperatures and three fatalities after anglers fell through thinning ice.

First ice is what people call ice when a body of water first freezes over. If it hasn't snowed, the ice is also called black ice. First ice may creak and groan—but not because you're walking on it. That is just the sound of ice fusing. It may also have natural cracks, which formed when the ice fused. These can actually help you gauge the depth of the ice. Know the difference between a dangerous sound (ice breaking) and a normal sound (ice fusing) and between a dangerous crack and a natural (safe) crack.

You have to be especially careful at first ice because the thickness may vary. As the season progresses, the ice

The appearance of the ice changes over the course of winter as you can see from the fishing holes on this page and the next page.

will turn to white marble ice. Eventually snow will cover the ice.

Late ice occurs in the spring. Rescues are especially common in the spring, as warmer days weaken the ice in some places. While ice is thickest by the shore during first ice, it's weakest by the shore during late ice.

Weather-wise, light snow is considered good for fishing, whereas fish tend to hide during heavy snowfalls. Warm fronts are considered good; cold fronts are considered bad. Stable weather is good. For all these fishing beliefs, you'll find that the best time to catch fish is whenever you catch fish. Nobody understands all the variables,

NEAR TRAGEDY ON THE ICE

Sometimes just following the rules and regulations isn't enough to keep people safe. Listening to warnings from experts is key, especially when it comes to ice fishing. In February 2022, the weather contributed to a dangerous situation on Lake Erie. Bitter cold followed by sunny skies created differences in the ice surface of the lake near northern Ohio. Weather officials warned that the conditions might create ice floes, or pieces of ice that break off. However, ice anglers, attracted to the nicer winter weather and perhaps not hearing the warnings, headed off across the lake. An ice floe separated from the shoreline and floated into the lake, trapping 18 people on it. (Snowmobile or ATV weight may have contributed to the break too.) Luckily, the U.S. Coast Guard, using an airboat and a helicopter, reached the fishers and safely got them to shore.

    These kinds of rescues are not uncommon as temperatures begin to warm toward spring. In fact, in 2009, 134 fishers were caught on an ice floe in the same area of Lake Erie. One died after his snowmobile broke through the ice.

    The U.S. Coast Guard cautions people to dress according to the temperature of the water, to always carry a life jacket, and to bring some kind of communications device when fishing, in case of emergency. Both the U.S. and Canadian Coast Guards and these countries' national weather services are resources to check about the safety of the ice in areas where you live.

and it's important to keep an open mind while still putting safety first.

THE BASICS OF TIP-UPS AND JIGS

When you have your spot on the ice, it's time to tip-up! The beauty of tip-ups is that you can set them up in various holes, and when you find a hot spot, move the other tip-ups nearby. Also, if you're with a group, all those baits tend to attract schools of panfish. If, on the other hand, fish are spooked by a large crowd, at a competition for instance, you may want to set tip-ups on the quieter side of the lake in hopes that the fish will flee from the crowd to you. For fish that are easily spooked, you may even want to watch the tip-ups from shore rather than on the ice.

The key to tip-up success is to focus on one type of fish. Cater your hook, line, and bait to that fish. Don't go for a trophy pike *and* some little fryers for dinner. You'll end up with neither. At the same time, be open-minded. A walleye presentation may result in an eelpout catch. When your flag goes up, pull the line in slowly by hand. Jerking it can cause you to lose the fish.

Although tip-ups allow you to have more lines on the ice, you'll likely catch more fish by jigging. You'll be better equipped to move the hook to different levels and to make the lure move. In the winter, slighter motions are better because fish don't work as hard for their food. For this same reason, bites may be light. Hold the line or use a bobber to detect the slightest hits.

The jig rod needs to be short so that you can muscle the fish out of the hole. For panfish, 18 to 26 inches (46 to 66 cm) is a good size, whereas you may need a 36- to 42-inch (91 to 107 cm) rod for game fish. Midsize

52　ICE FISHING LIKE A PRO

Panfish may have got their name because they're the perfect size to cook in a pan over a campfire.

fish will require something in between. Cater the lure to the species—light-tipped for panfish and bigger with more action for game fish.

When you catch the fish, there are two schools of thought: Hook it while it runs or wait until it stops. The latter is the point when the fish eats the bait, so the hook should be firmly in its mouth. Tug the line to place the hook, then reel it in!

CHAPTER 4
FINDING YOUR FISH

Which do you see yourself hoping to reel in on the ice, panfish or game fish? Don't discount panfish. Though many do fit in a pan, some can grow to be tasty trophy fish. For instance, the world ice-fishing tip-up record for yellow perch (a popular ice-fishing panfish) is 2 pounds 11.68 ounces (1.2 kg). (That was set in 2014 in Idaho by an 11-year-old fisher.) More commonly, yellow perch weigh less than 1 pound (454 g). Panfish feed on plankton, which are tiny water-dwelling organisms, aquatic insects, and very small fish such as minnows. Panfish are prey for bigger fish so they're an important part of a habitat's food web.

PURSUING PANFISH

Panfish are the most common target of ice fishers. And it's no wonder. Panfish are plentiful in most waters, including rivers, backwaters, ponds, lakes, and bays. They're abundant breeders. If their numbers exceed their food supply, they're easy to catch but small and of poor quality. In a more balanced lake, they're less plentiful but a better quality. Below are tips for catching specific types of panfish.

BLUEGILLS

This member of the sunfish family prefers to feed in the late afternoon and evening. They're enthusiastic biters, so if you find them, you'll likely catch them. They eat plankton, so your lures should be small—even flies work well. For bait, they like wax worms or maggots.

CRAPPIES

Crappies are also a kind of sunfish and one of the most commonly caught fish in the Northeast and Canada, with the black crappie being more common than the white

FINDING YOUR FISH   57

Some anglers suggest attaching a glowstick to the lure to attract crappies at night. Check regulations before you do, though.

58 ICE FISHING LIKE A PRO

Schooling behavior can make it easy to catch a number of fish on one outing.

(though they look a lot alike). Crappies like to live somewhere between the shallow waters and the deepest waters, often around 20 feet (6 m) down in mid-winter. However, they may be found close to the surface after first ice and late ice as well as before a storm. They like to hide among structures and weeds but may be in open water too. The best time to catch them is in the evening, but especially dusk and dawn. If you're able to tell where the crappies are, lower your bait to above their eye level, as their eyes are positioned for upfeeding. Jig for them with a medium-sized minnow on a double hook, and give them plenty of line, as resistance causes them to drop the bait. You'll be glad if the crappies are biting. They taste great!

YELLOW PERCH

Yellow perch are found everywhere. They're a good fish to seek when you're making a day of ice fishing because they feed during daylight. Because their schools number 50 to 200 fish, you can catch a lot in a short time. While they school with like-sized fish, you might find larger perch on the outer edge of the school. Within their body of water, they like channels, rocky points, and drop-offs—they can be found 40 feet (12 m) or more deep. They're likely to stay put for days, so ask other fishers where they're biting. Larger yellow perch eat small fish, so use a minnow as bait or a swimming lure such as the 1.5-inch (4 cm) Swedish pimple.

WHITE PERCH

This "perch" is really a bass. It's not called a white bass because another bass is already named that. In fact, the two species sometimes mate, creating a hybrid. Native to Quebec, New England, and New York, the white perch has invaded the Great Lakes, threatening the walleye population by eating its eggs. White perch are good to eat, and if you fish for them in the Great Lakes, you'll be doing your part to save the walleyes. White perch can be caught at dusk along muck-bottom flats 15 to 30 feet (4.6 to 9 m) deep. Small minnows work well as bait.

STOCKED TROUT

Alpine lakes and mountain reservoirs are home to trophy trout, so you might want to fish for them as you would for game fish, with heavier lines and bigger bait. But stocked trout are often smaller. You can check with your state or local fisheries department for information about which lakes are stocked with trout. Trout feed during the early morning, at twilight, and on gloomy days. A spinning lure tipped with bait works well, and for bait, they like wax worms, night crawlers, minnows, and shrimp.

KOKANEE SALMON

Most salmon species are considered game fish, but kokanee salmon are smaller. They don't migrate to the ocean to feed and therefore don't grow as large as other salmon. Don't let their size fool you, though: They fight hard when caught—and they're hard to catch. Typically found in the western United States, kokanee can best be snagged with a light line, smaller hook, and small bait or a flashy lure.

SMELT

Perhaps it doesn't have the best name for a fish, but smelt is tasty. In fact, even though it's small enough to be used as bait, smelt is still the most popular catch at some lakes, including Lake Champlain and Lake George. Smelts often

FINDING YOUR FISH 61

Trout like to hunt for food in shallow flats. These are areas of shallow water with a mostly flat bottom.

You see from this angler's catch that smelts can be a variety of sizes. Some can be used as bait and others as dinner.

congregate in the same places each year, so talking to other fishers is helpful. However, invasive species and changing lakes can force smelts into new habitats, which has happened at Lake Champlain. Traditionally, anglers use a large-diameter spool nailed to a wall of an ice shack to catch smelts. The presentation is similar to what you'd use to catch yellow perch. A bobber indicates when you have a bite. Then the line is reeled in by hand. You can also jig for smelts.

GETTING YOUR GAME FISH

Game fish aren't just large. They're also thought to be more fun to catch because their strength makes the angler fight to bring them in. Game fish eat panfish, and so they're often found where panfish are found. However, you need a heavier line, bigger hook, and bigger bait to catch game fish, so it's hard to catch both types of fish with one rod. Another difference is that while you can find good panfish in a small but well-balanced body of water, game fish in these places tend to be small and of poor quality. If you want to catch big fish, you should go to larger waters. Popular winter game fish are walleye, eelpout, pike, bass, trout, and salmon. Here are tips for catching each species.

WALLEYE

The walleye is known for the glassy appearance of its eyes, which can appear to be silvery or transparent when in the light. It's the state fish of Minnesota, where anglers bring home about 3.5 million walleyes every year—the Mille Lacs region alone can sustain a harvest of 100,300 pounds (45,495 kg) of walleye.

Regulations limit the number and size of walleyes that can be kept, so many are released. The walleye's popularity is no mystery. It provides thick white fillets and presents a challenge to anglers. (Sauger is similar to walleye but smaller and less common. Both fish can be caught using similar methods.)

Walleye hold up in deep dark water by day and feed in shallows at twilight and night. The best place to catch them is around irregular features that lead from the shallows to deep water. Vegetation, channel edges, and shoals are good bets—and walleye like a strong current. But walleye fishing requires patience. A few days of no feeding can be followed by a bite, so don't give up.

As with all game fish, jigging is a good way to find walleyes. A tip-up with a minnow next to your jigging hole may attract the walleye to your jig pole, on which you can use a minnow-imitating lure. The walleye is a wary fish, so a light line—6-pound (3 kg) test—is necessary. Slowly lower and raise the line. When you hook the fish, pull it up steadily, giving it line when it runs. This is especially necessary near the hole, where most walleye are lost.

Many anglers fish for walleye on big rivers, such as the Fox, Wisconsin, Wolf, Mississippi, Rainy, and Saginaw. Backwaters and locks adjoining dams are especially good.

EELPOUT

Anglers often catch eelpout when they're seeking walleye, so the fish is seen by some walleye anglers as a disappointment. But others shouldn't feel this way. It's true that eelpout are rather ugly. But most people don't catch fish for their looks but for their taste, and eelpout—also

FINDING YOUR FISH   65

Effective live bait for walleye are night crawlers, minnows, and leeches.

SPEARFISHING

Spearfishing is the act of hunting fish using a speargun or polespear. In warmer weather, spear fishers may enter the water. This isn't possible for ice fishing, of course. Ice fishers may use an ice spear. It has five to seven barbed points at the end of a long metal pole. Some have tips that detach. A rope allows the fisher to throw the spear and retrieve it, hopefully with a fish attached. Popular targets to spearfish are northern pike, sturgeon, catfish, and lake whitefish.

Spearfishing is best done in shallower waters. Cut a large rectangular hole, perhaps by drilling several holes and using an ice saw. Some places have regulations about how big an ice hole can be, so do your research. After the hole is prepared, cover it with a windowless shelter called a dark house. (If you're running a heater, be sure to have ventilation.) Your eyes will adjust to the dark, and you'll be able to see the fish below. Drop a flashy decoy tied to a string into the water. This could be a store-bought decoy or a spoon attached to a pole. When a fish comes along to investigate, identify it to be sure it's a legal catch. Then, put the points of the spear into the water slowly. Finally, aim behind the head of the fish and throw—don't stab. Hopefully, you'll spear your dinner.

As of February 2023, ice spearfishing was legal in eight states: Minnesota, Michigan, North Dakota, South Dakota, Colorado, Montana, Vermont, and Alaska. (Some states allow spearfishing in salt water but not fresh water. And some may require a special license too, so check out the regulations in your state first.) Wisconsin allows ice spearfishing for sturgeon for just 16 days each year on Lake Winnebago—or until the caps, or limits, for sturgeon have been met in order to protect this species. In Canada, some provinces, including Quebec, allow ice spearfishing but only for certain species.

known as burbot, ling, freshwater cod, lawyer, and poor man's lobster—can be delicious.

Early ice is the period before eelpout spawn. At this time, they're in deep waters. They go deeper later in the season—as deep as 700 feet (213 m). In mid-winter, though, they come to shallow waters to spawn. Your best bet is to arrive in the afternoon to drill various holes

Adult eelpout eat mostly other fish such as small yellow perch and walleyes.

along a steep-breaking structure that you think eelpout will follow. Just after dark, the fish will begin to move along the structure and hopefully bite.

Shiny lures tipped with minnows work well on tip-ups. For your jig pole, use a glow-in-the-dark jig head and live bait. Eelpout bait needs to be fresh, so change it about every 15 minutes. Because it's nighttime, you can use a heavy line without spooking the eelpout. You should hold the line just off the bottom. When you catch an eelpout, be prepared for it to dive as it fights for freedom.

PIKE

Known as the Great White of the North, the pike is the top predator of northern lakes and usually grows to be 2 to 30 pounds (0.9 to 14 kg). It feeds from sunup to noon, lurking in shallow water with weed beds. Live bait on a jig works best, and heavy line is necessary. When you hook one, you may have to let it run several times as it approaches the hole. Finally, you should be able to grab it by the gills and pull it in. Watch out, though—pike have sharp teeth!

Pike have white, flaky meat. They're considered by some to be bony, but you can get five fillets off a 24-inch (61 cm) long pike.

SMALLMOUTH AND LARGEMOUTH BASS

After first ice, largemouth bass move into deeper waters for a month or two, feeding among deeper weed beds. Then they come up looking for more food. However, they have less energy this time of year. They don't attack bait like

PREPARING A PIKE

If you're hoping to eat your pike rather than release it, you might want to know how to get it ready for the frying pan. Even in cold weather, make sure you keep it on ice until it's time to fillet it. When you're ready, set it down on its belly. First, with a very sharp knife (be careful!), cut behind the head, perpendicular to the spine, until the blade touches the spine. Then, turn the knife toward the tail and cut the meat off the back of the fish. This should give you a back fillet. You should be able to see three bones running down the back. You can get a fillet off each side of these. Lay the fish on its side and make a cut perpendicular to its back at the head and a similar cut on its anal fin. Then cut from front to back along the ribs. For two more fillets, make a perpendicular cut just behind its anus and slide your knife to its tail fin. Turn over, and repeat these cuts.

To remove the skin, bring water to a boil and pour it over the fillets before skinning. (Pike skin can be difficult to remove.) Wash and salt the fillets. Dip each in flour, and shake off the excess. Fry them in heated oil, and enjoy eating your catch!

they would in the summer. A light tug on a hook tipped with a wax worm might be enough to interest a bass.

While largemouth bass will seek out shallow water in mid-winter, smallmouth bass go deep. Experts suggest aiming at humps, rock piles, and reefs 20 to 30 feet (6 to 9 m) deep. Electronics and maps will help with finding structures like this. The jigging can be the same for smallmouth bass as largemouth, but smallmouth are usually looking for a bigger meal, such as minnows.

TROUT

Native to northern United States and Canada, lake trout prefer cold water and live in deep bodies such as Lake Superior and the Canadian Shield lakes. They're also found in

When bringing up a fish from deep waters, try not to cause it barotrauma if you plan to release it. Release the fish back into the water as quickly as possible. Or, if you plan on catching and releasing, only do it in shallow waters.

deep freshwater rivers that run into these bodies of water. In the summer, they go very deep, where the water is colder. But in winter, all depths are cold, so they can be found at mid-depth—20 to 50 feet (6 to 15 m) deep. They're often found alone instead of in schools. Lure them with bright colors, and use a sucker or chub minnow for bait.

Brown trout is a beautiful fish native to Europe and Asia but was introduced to American waters. It's typically 12 to 22 inches (30 to 56 cm) when caught. They're hungriest during low-light periods, but will come up throughout the day. Bait to hook a brown trout includes minnows, leeches, wax worms, and crickets.

SALMON

Catching winter salmon is rare along the southern edge of the ice belt because they need very cold, oxygenated water. Such waters, like the deep parts of the Great Lakes, seldom freeze. Some deepwater bays of Lakes Superior and Huron support ice fishing for salmon, however. And farther north, in places such as Alaska, salmon are one of the primary species to ice fish.

Salmon can be big and strong, so use a heavy line, as much as 20-pound (9 kg) test monofilament, and a swimming lure tipped with a smelt, shiner, or minnow. When you hook a salmon, be prepared for it to fight for up to an hour before it lets you pull it from the hole!

HONEY HOLES AND TIGHT LINES

If you do catch fish, remember your location! It may be a honey hole, or a spot you can return to for consistent action. Share your luck with other anglers, and they will return the favor with their favorite lucky spots. You might

72 ICE FISHING LIKE A PRO

Even the smallest catch brings big smiles to an ice angler's face. Don't forget small catches can make good bait too!

even want to write in a fishing journal to keep track of what you learn on each expedition. (This is also a good way to spend time and stay patient next to your hole during those hours between tugs on your line or tip-up.)

Once you feel the magic of ice fishing, you'll have an activity that will get you excited for the winter months. You'll know the ice angler's secret—you don't feel the cold when the line tenses and you've got a fish on the hook. And laughing and chatting with friends on the ice is a perfect way to spend a few hours during the colder, darker months of the year.

Many experienced fishers believe that saying "good luck" to another fisher actually brings bad luck. Instead, they wish each other "tight lines" on the ice. Hopefully, the tips, guidelines, and strategies in this book will bring you and your fishing friends tight lines on the hard water for winters to come!

GLOSSARY

auger: A large corkscrew apparatus turned either manually or through gas or electric power to drill holes in ice.

barotrauma: Harm to the body because of changes in pressure.

Canadian Shield: Plateau area of eastern Canada and the northeastern United States, from the Mackenzie River basin east to Davis Strait and south to southern Quebec, northeastern Minnesota, northern Wisconsin, northwestern Michigan, and northeastern New York.

decoy: A fake fish used to attract live fish.

frostbite: Tissue damage—sometimes permanent—caused by exposure to cold.

GPS: Stands for global positioning system. A navigation system that shows people where they are in relation to satellite-based maps.

graphite: A kind of material in which carbon fibers are the reinforcing matter.

hypothermia: Lowered body temperature that can be caused by exposure to cold and can lead to health emergencies.

invasive species: One kind of living thing likely to spread and be harmful when placed in a new area.

jet stream: A long strong current of winds high above Earth's surface, often blowing from a westerly direction.

jig: A lure that moves in the water by way of the angler moving the pole. A jig also refers to the pole itself and the act of fishing with this type of pole.

lure: A nonfood object placed at the end of a fishing line to attract fish.

monofilament: A type of fishing line made from a single, untwisted strand of material, often nylon.

phosphorescent: Able to give off light after being exposed to radiation.

presentation: In fishing, any combination of line, hook, lure, and bait that is visible to fish.

wax worm: A worm that is the larva of the wax moth.

For Further Reading

Bolt Simons, Lisa M. *Go Freshwater Fishing!* North Mankato, MN: Capstone Press, 2022.

Doyle, Abby Badach. *Ice Fishing*. Buffalo, NY: Gareth Stevens Publishing, 2023.

Hogan, Zeb, and Stefan Lovgren. *Chasing Giants: In Search of the World's Largest Freshwater Fish*. Reno, NV: University of Nevada Press, 2023.

Katirgis, Jane, and Judy Monroe Peterson. *Insider Tips for Fishing in Lakes and Ponds*. New York, NY: Rosen Publishing, 2020.

Mazzarella, Kerri. *Ice Fishing*. New York, NY: Crabtree Publishing Company, 2023.

Mazzarella, Kerri. *Spearfishing*. New York, NY: Crabtree Publishing Company, 2023.

Reeves, Diane Lindsey. *Freshwater Fishing*. Minneapolis, MN: Lerner Publications, 2024.

Underwood, Lamar, ed. *1001 Fishing Tips: The Ultimate Guide to Finding and Catching More and Bigger Fish*. New York, NY: Skyhorse Publishing, 2022.

Werner, Robert G. *Freshwater Fishes of the Northeastern United States: A Field Guide*. Syracuse, NY: Syracuse University Press, 2023.

For More Information

American Sportfishing Association
1001 North Fairfax Street, Suite 501
Alexandria, VA 22314
(703) 519-9691
Email: info@asafishing.org
Website: www.asafishing.org
Twitter: @ASAFishing
Facebook: /ASAfishing/
The American Sportfishing Association represents the interests of sport fishers, including ice anglers, and fishing businesses.

Brainerd Jaycees Ice Fishing Extravaganza
Hole-in-the-Day Bay
Gull Lake, Minnesota
Contact form: icefishing.org/contact/
Email: chair@icefishing.org
Website: icefishing.org/
Twitter: @IceExtravaganza
Facebook: /TheExtravaganza/
The Brainerd Jaycees Ice Fishing Extravaganza was established over 30 years ago. It has grown to be one of the biggest charitable ice-fishing contests in the world.

Fisheries and Oceans Canada
200 Kent Street
Station 15N100
Ottawa, ON K1A 0E6
Canada
(613) 993-0999
Email: info@dfo-mpo.gc.ca
Website:www.dfo-mpo.gc.ca/
Twitter: @FishOceansCAN
Facebook: /FisheriesOceansCanada
This is the federal institution responsible for managing Canadian fisheries and ocean resources. Look for links to ice-fishing information for the provinces.

The International Game Fish Association (IGFA)
300 Gulf Stream Way
Dania Beach, FL 33004
(954) 927-2628
Email: hq@igfa.org
Website: www.igfa.org
Twitter: @TheIGFA
Facebook: /International-Game-Fish-Association/
The IGFA is the worldwide authority on sportfishing. It also keeps the world records of game fishing.

Islands Ice Fishing Derby
2934 VT Route 2
Highgate Springs, VT 05460
Email: islandsderby@gmail.com
Website: www.islandsderby.com/
Facebook: /islandsicefishingderby/
For more than 40 years, this ice-fishing competition has taken place on Lake Champlain in Vermont.

Mille Lacs Area Tourism
P.O. Box 286
Isle, MN 56342
(888) 350-2692
Email: vacation@millelacs.com
Website: millelacs.com
Twitter: @MilleLacTourism
Facebook: /MilleLacsAreaTourism/
The Mille Lacs Area Tourism Council provides facts about visiting the Mille Lacs Lake area. Find information about the ice-fishing season.

U.S. Fish and Wildlife Service
1849 C Street NW
Washington, D.C. 20240
(800) 344-WILD (1-800-344-9453)
Website: www.fws.gov
Twitter: @USFWS
Facebook: /USFWS/
The U.S. Fish and Wildlife Service is the federal agency responsible for the management and conservation of fish, wildlife, and habitats.

INDEX

A
Alaska, 5, 12, 66, 71
auger, 16, 17, 26, 27, 28

B
bait, 5, 30, 31, 32, 42, 51, 53, 59, 60, 63, 65, 68, 70, 71 72
bass, 5, 59, 60, 63, 68, 69, 70
bluegill, 56

C
California, 8
Canada, 5, 8, 10, 11, 13, 23, 37, 42, 50, 56, 66, 70
catfish, 66
chisel, 16, 26
climate change, 47
cod, 13
Colorado, 11, 12, 66
crappies, 56, 57, 59

D
depth finder, 38

E
eelpout, 51, 63, 64, 67, 68

G
gaff, 32, 43
Genz, Dave, 36
GPS, 38, 39, 47
Great Lakes, 8, 10, 11, 18, 50, 60, 70, 71

H
hook, 4, 28, 31, 32, 42, 43, 51, 53, 63, 69, 73
hypothermia, 18, 20

I
ice belt, 8
ice conditions, 4, 5, 8, 14, 16, 18, 19, 20, 21, 26, 47, 48, 49, 50
Idaho, 8, 56

J
jigging rods, 28, 51, 64

L
leader, 30
license, 42, 43, 66
line, 23, 28, 30, 31, 32, 51, 53, 59, 63, 64, 68, 73
lure, 28, 30, 31, 32, 42, 60, 64

M
Maine, 11
Michigan, 8, 10, 46, 66
Minnesota, 5, 8, 9, 10, 21, 36, 63, 66
Montana, 11, 66

N
Nebraska, 8
New Mexico, 8
New York, 10, 59
North Dakota, 11, 66

O

Ohio, 50

P

panfish, 5, 8, 10, 26, 28, 31, 32, 46, 51, 52, 53, 56, 63
Pennsylvania, 8
perch, 5, 8, 13, 46, 56, 59, 60, 63, 67
pike, 5, 28, 51, 63, 66, 68, 69

R

redfish, 13
rod, 4, 23, 28, 29, 30, 37, 51, 63, 64

S

safety, 4, 5, 8, 13, 14, 15, 16, 18, 19, 20, 26, 39, 48, 50
salmon, 5, 10, 12, 60, 63, 71
shelters, 5, 10, 11, 14, 18, 34, 35, 36, 37, 44, 63, 66
skimmer, 28
smelt, 13, 46, 62, 63, 71
sonar, 4, 38, 46
South Dakota, 11, 66
spearfishing, 4, 5, 10, 23, 38, 66
spud bar, 16, 26, 27
sturgeon, 5, 10, 66

T

tip-ups, 30, 31, 42, 50, 56, 64, 68, 73
trout, 5, 11, 12, 28, 60, 61, 63, 70, 71

U

Utah, 11

V

vehicles, 14, 15, 32, 39, 50
Vermont, 47, 66

W

walleye, 5, 8, 46, 51, 60, 63, 64, 65, 67
Washington, 8
Wisconsin, 5, 8, 10, 23, 66
Wyoming, 11

ABOUT THE AUTHOR

Marie Roesser has been an avid angler since she was four years old. A lover of all things nature, she's the catch-and-release champion of her local saltwater fishing club and the secretary of her town's conservation society. When not on the water, Roesser can be found in her garden or on her bike. She lives in East Sandwich, Massachusetts.

ABOUT THE CONSULTANT

Contributor Benjamin Cowan has more than 20 years of both freshwater and saltwater angling experience. In addition to being an avid outdoorsman, Cowan is a member of many conservation organizations. He currently resides in western Tennessee.

PHOTO CREDITS

Cover schankz/Shutterstock.com; pp. 4-5 divedog/Shutterstock.com; pp. 6-7 Beth Harvey/Shutterstock.com; p. 9 Per-Boge/Shutterstock.com; p. 10 Daniel Toh/Shutterstock.com; p. 12 CSNafzger/Shutterstock.com; p. 13 Pierre Williot/Shutterstock.com; p. 15 Tyler Olsen/Shutterstock.com; p. 17 Stephen Mcsweeny/Shutterstock.com; p. 19 Elena Berd/Shutterstock.com; 21 Neil Liesenfeld/Shutterstock.com; p. 22 Mark Agnor/Shutterstock.com; pp. 24-25 PRESSLAB/Shutterstock.com; p. 27 Maxim Petrichuk/Shutterstock.com; p. 29 AlisLuch/Shutterstock.com; p. 30 Moiseenko Maksim/Shutterstock.com; p. 31 Aleron Val/Shutterstock.com; p. 33 Ramon Cliff/Shutterstock.com; p. 34 Splingis/Shutterstock.com; p. 35 Joseph Kreiss/Shutterstock.com; p. 37 Pinkcandy/Shutterstock.com; pp. 40-41 Hero Images Inc./Alamy Stock Photo; p. 43 Lisa Schulz/Shutterstock.com; p. 44 joojoob27/Shutterstock.com; p. 45 O. Kemppainen/Shutterstock.com; p. 48 John Danow/Shutterstock.com; p. 49 Bragapictures/Shutterstock.com; p. 52 michasekdzi/Shutterstock.com; pp. 54-55 Alex Erofeenkov/Shutterstock.com; p. 57 dcwcreations/Shutterstock.com; p. 58 Alexander Lukatskiy/Shutterstock.com; p. 61 Piotr Wawrzyniuk/Shutterstock.com; p. 62 Kirsanov Valeriy Vladimirovich/Shutterstock.com; p. 65 dcwcreations/Shutterstock.com; p. 67 Sergei Gorlanov/Shutterstock.com; p. 70 michasekdzi/Shutterstock.com; p. 72 Dudarev Mikhail/Shutterstock.com.